LOCOMOTION!

MARCH, HOP, SKIP, GALLOP, RUN

By MICHAEL DAHL

Illustrations by BETH HUGHES

Music by MARK MALLMAN

CANTATA
LEARNING

WWW.CANTATALEARNING.COM

CANTATA LEARNING

Published by Cantata Learning
1710 Roe Crest Drive
North Mankato, MN 56003
www.cantatalearning.com

Library of Congress Cataloging-in-Publication Data
Library of Congress Cataloging-in-Publication Data

Names: Dahl, Michael, author. | Hughes, Beth, illustrator. | Mallman, Mark,
    composer.
Title: Locomotion! : march, hop, skip, gallop, run / by Michael Dahl ;
    illustrations by Beth Hughes ; music by Mark Mallman.
Description: North Mankato, MN : Cantata Learning, 2019. | Series: Creative
    movement | Audience: K to Grade 3.
Identifiers: LCCN 2017056291 | ISBN 9781684102433 (hardcover : alk. paper) |
    ISBN 9781684102686 (ebook)
Subjects: LCSH: Human locomotion--Juvenile literature.
Classification: LCC QP301 .D244 2018 | DDC 612.7/6--dc23
LC record available at https://lccn.loc.gov/2017056291

Book design and art direction, Tim Palin Creative
Editorial direction, Kellie M. Hultgren
Music direction, Elizabeth Draper
Music arranged and produced by Mark Mallman

Printed in the United States of America.
0390

ACCESS THE MUSIC!

SCAN CODE WITH MOBILE APP

CANTATALEARNING.COM

TIPS TO SUPPORT LITERACY AT HOME

WHY READING AND SINGING WITH YOUR CHILD IS SO IMPORTANT

Daily reading with your child leads to increased academic achievement. Music and songs, specifically rhyming songs, are a fun and easy way to build early literacy and language development. Music skills correlate significantly with both phonological awareness and reading development. Singing helps build vocabulary and speech development. And reading and appreciating music together is a wonderful way to strengthen your relationship.

READ AND SING EVERY DAY!

TIPS FOR USING CANTATA LEARNING BOOKS AND SONGS DURING YOUR DAILY STORY TIME

1. As you sing and read, point out the different words on the page that rhyme. Suggest other words that rhyme.

2. Memorize simple rhymes such as Itsy Bitsy Spider and sing them together. This encourages comprehension skills and early literacy skills.

3. Use the questions in the back of each book to guide your singing and storytelling.

4. Read the included sheet music with your child while you listen to the song. How do the music notes correlate to the words of the song?

5. Sing along on the go and at home. Access music by scanning the QR code on each Cantata book. You can also stream or download the music for free to your computer, smartphone, or mobile device.

Devoting time to daily reading shows that you are available for your child. Together, you are building language, literacy, and listening skills.

Have fun reading and singing!

We all move every day as we go from one place to another. We move around our rooms, our homes, and our classrooms. We move from inside to outside and back again. And then we stop.

But there are so many different ways we can move! Turn the page to get in motion and move along to the song!

5

Get in the groove! Let's all move
arms and legs in cool **commotion**!

Loco! **Locomotion**!
Loco! Locomotion!

Arms move back and forth.
Legs go up and down.

March, march, march!
Let's march around the town.

Go, go, go! Make a mighty motion!
March, march, march! Loco! Locomotion!

Arms swing low, then high.
Feet jump in the air.

Hop, hop, hop!
Let's hop from here to there.

Arms swing up and down.
Feet hop-step along.

Skip, skip, skip!
Let's skip and sing our song!

Go, go, go! Make a mighty motion!
Skip, skip, skip! Loco! Locomotion!

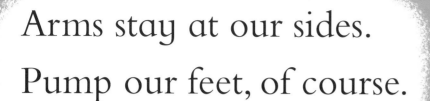

Arms stay at our sides.
Pump our feet, of course.

Gallop, gallop, gallop!
Let's gallop like a horse.

14

Go, go, go! Make a mighty motion!
Gallop! Gallop! Gallop! Loco! Locomotion!

Feet go faster now.

Pump your arms and knees.

Run, run, run!

Run faster than the breeze!

Go, go, go! Make a mighty motion!
Run, run, run! Loco! Locomotion!

Slow our running down.
Gallop to a stop.

Slowly skip. Slowly hop.
We march then slowly drop.

Slow, slow, slow.

We made a mighty motion.

Get down low.

Stay low for low commotion!

SONG LYRICS
Locomotion! March, Hop, Skip, Gallop, Run

Get in the groove!
    Let's all move
arms and legs in cool commotion!

Loco! Locomotion!
Loco! Locomotion!

Arms move back and forth.
Legs go up and down.

March, march, march!
Let's march around the town.

Go, go, go! Make a mighty motion!
March, march, march! Loco!
    Locomotion!

Arms swing low, then high.
Feet jump in the air.

Hop, hop, hop!
Let's hop from here to there.

Go, go, go! Make a mighty motion!
Hop, hop, hop! Loco! Locomotion!

Arms swing up and down.
Feet hop-step along.

Skip, skip, skip!
Let's skip and sing our song!

Go, go, go! Make a mighty motion!
Skip, skip, skip! Loco! Locomotion!

Arms stay at our sides.
Pump our feet, of course.

Gallop, gallop, gallop!
Let's gallop like a horse.

Go, go, go! Make a mighty motion!
Gallop! Gallop! Gallop! Loco!
    Locomotion!

Feet go faster now.
Pump your arms and knees.

Run, run, run!
Run faster than the breeze!

Go, go, go! Make a mighty motion!
Run, run, run! Loco! Locomotion!

Slow our running down.
Gallop to a stop.

Slowly skip. Slowly hop.
We march then slowly drop.

Slow, slow, slow.
We made a mighty motion.

Get down low.
Stay low for low commotion!

Locomotion! March, Hop, Skip, Gallop, Run

Latin Pop
Mark Mallman

Verse 2
Arms swing low, then high.
Feet jump in the air.
Hop, hop, hop!
Let's hop from here to there.

Chorus

Verse 3
Arms swing up and down.
Feet hop-step along.
Skip, skip, skip!
Let's skip and sing our song!

Chorus

Verse 4
Arms stay at our sides.
Pump our feet, of course.
Gallop, gallop, gallop!
Let's gallop like a horse.

Chorus
(tempo change)

Verse 5
Feet go faster now.
Pump your arms and knees.
Run, run, run!
Run faster than the breeze!

Chorus
(tempo change)

Verse 6
Slow our running down.
Gallop to a stop.
Slowly skip. Slowly hop.
We march then slowly drop.

GLOSSARY

commotion—lots of noise and movement

gallop—move fast, with one foot always leading and the other following

hop—jump up and down, with both feet or on one foot

locomotion—moving in a special way

march—walk steadily, lifting knees and elbows high

skip—move lightly by stepping forward and then hopping

CRITICAL THINKING QUESTIONS

1. This book shows five ways you can move. Can you march and hop at the same time? Can you hop and gallop?

2. When you gallop, you move like a horse. Can you move like a different animal? Do small animals and big animals move in different ways?

3. The motions in this book all use your feet. Can you show the different ways to move by using just your hands?

TO LEARN MORE

Gates, Mariam. *Good Morning Yoga: A Pose-by-Pose Wake Up Story*. Louisville, CO: Sounds True, 2016.

Hoena, Blake. *Stretchy Shapes! Straight, Curved, and Twisty*. North Mankato, MN: Cantata Learning, 2019.

Hopwood, Lolly, and YoYo Kusters. *Move!* New York: Workman, 2016.

Jenkins, Steve, and Robin Page. *Flying Frogs and Walking Fish*. New York: HMH Books for Young Readers, 2016.

Russo, Brian. *Yoga Bunny*. New York: HarperCollins, 2016.